CW00556121

All rights for this book here presented belong exclusively to the authors. Use or reproduction of the text is forbidden and requires clear consent of the authors.

Please note. That the recipes cooking times are approximate and depend largely on the amount of servings you are preparing for. This goes without saying but feel free to adjust where necessary.

Food Photography
By Andre Small & Michael Mcken

Portrait photography
by Andrea Crab

EATING GOOD VEGAN

DELICIOUS PLANTBASED AND CARIBBEAN INSPIRED RECIPES BY ANDRE SMALL & MICHAEL MCKEN

We want to take a moment to thank our mothers & all our ancestors who came before us, that have allowed us to soak in their culinary genius. We humbly thank you and will do our best to pave a lane for those that come after us.

Contents

DRINKS

Hello

We're super excited that you've bought this book. Why? Because we're almost certain that each recipe is going to take you on an adventure filled with flavor.

We also wanted to use this opportunity to say hello! We're Michael and Andre, two vegans from the UK who are always trying to bring more flavor and creativity to your plate.

Both of us have been vegan for over 5 years and one thing we like to do most is to veganise some

of our old favorites from our meat-eating days. What that means is, we're certain that whether you're vegan or not, you and your family will love these recipes. Both of us have Caribbean roots, so you won't be surprised that many dishes in this book will be bursting with Caribbean flavors.

Let's be honest, a lot of the time, vegan food gets a bad rap. Just a salad? No flavor or poor texture? We don't subscribe to this, and this book was designed to help you see this for what it truly is - a lie! Trust us when we say, vegan food has come a long way.

We've created a FaceBook group for you to join, scan the QR code below and come and say hello, we'd love to keep in touch with you and answer any questions you might have.

Big Love,

Michael & Andre

Brunch

The majority of our **passion for cooking** comes from seeing our mothers cook from scratch and learning basic skills from them. They always managed to make a delicious meal from even the most basic ingredients, nothing posh or fancy, with no measuring whatsoever. But the outcome was always the same, full of flavour and love. We have wrapped and sealed that exact same **passion and energy** into our brunch recipes. We would love to hear your experiences with our recipes and we hope it brings you **joy and satisfaction.**

Banana Fritters

SERVES: 3   **COOK TIME:** 30 MINUTES   **DIFFICULTY:** ● ●

One of our more addictive recipes. It's lip smackingly good, from its fluffy exterior to mouthwatering aftertaste. This can be paired with a variety of different toppings, from banana slices, frozen berries to nut butter. You will be happy to find they are also perfect alone whilst you take that cheeky first bite while cooking.

INGREDIENTS

5 ripe banana

1 tbsp cinnamon

1 ½ tsp nutmeg

1 tbsp vanilla extract

1 tsp salt

194 g/1 cup brown sugar

250 g/2 cups flour

4 tbsp oil for frying

DIRECTIONS

Peel the bananas and place them in a large mixing bowl. Using a fork or a potato masher, mash the banana's until pureed and smooth.

Add cinnamon, nutmeg, vanilla extract, sugar and salt to the mixing bowl and combine together with mashed banana.

Add the flour to the mixture one cup at a time, mixing in between each cup.

In a non-stick skillet, add enough oil to shallow fry and bring to a medium heat.

Using a large serving spoon, add a scoop of the banana mixture into the hot oil and leave to cook until golden brown, flip halfway through to cook on both sides.

When cooked, transfer onto a plate covered with kitchen towel to drain any excess oil.

Eat on it's own or serve with your favourite pancake toppings, such as nut butter, maple syrup, and cinnamon.

GOT A QUESTION ?

BLT & Plantain

SERVES: 2   **COOK TIME:** 45 MINUTES   **DIFFICULTY:** ● ●

Inspired by Gordon Ramsay's vegan bacon (UK Chef), we've remixed this crowd favourite and brought you a BLT that is a hit in any house. Crispy flavoursome bacon pieces, alongside golden brown plantain with sliced avocado. I'm certain this will soon be a favourite in your home.

INGREDIENTS

100g extra-firm tofu, drained and pressed

4 tbsp nutritional yeast

2 tbsp vegan Sriracha

1 tbsp garlic powder

1 tsp pimento powder

1 tsp all-purpose seasoning

½ tsp cayenne pepper

½ tbsp smoked paprika

2 tsp liquid smoke

¼ cup /60ml pure maple syrup

3 tbsp soy sauce or tamari

4 tbsp vegan butter, melted

3 tbsp water

5 sheets rice paper

1 ripe plantain, sliced and fried

1 avocado, sliced

1 tomato, sliced

lettuce

sourdough bread, sliced and toasted

DIRECTIONS

Preheat oven to 190°C/ 375°F.

In a large bowl, prepare the marinade for bacon by combining 2 tbsp nutritional yeast, sriracha garlic powder, pimento powder, all-purpose seasoning, cayenne pepper, smoked paprika, liquid smoke, maple syrup, soy sauce and melted vegan butter. Mix together well then set aside.

In another bowl, crumble your tofu into small pieces using your hands. Add 2 tbsp nutritional yeast followed by 3 tbsp of your marinade then set aside.

To prepare bacon strips, using kitchen scissors cut rice paper into 1 ½ inch wide strips. Dip rice paper one by one into marinade and coat well. Then place one coated rice paper onto a lined baking tray. Place marinated tofu on rice paper strip so that it looks similar to fat on bacon. Dip another rice paper strip into marinade coating well and then place on top of the first strip with tofu. Fuse strips together as well as you can, however it doesn't matter if they don't stick to begin with. Repeat process with remaining strips. Put strips to bake for 10 minutes. Once baked, allow to cool for a couple of minutes.

To assemble, butter toasted bread, add sliced tomatoes, followed by lettuce, bacon strips, fried plantain and avocado, top with other slice of bread.

GOT A QUESTION ? ——»

Vegan Saltfish & Callaloo

SERVES: 3　　　**COOK TIME:** 45 MINUTES　　　**DIFFICULTY:** ● ●

INGREDIENTS

400 g/ 1 can (12 oz) banana blossom, minced

3 tsp garlic powder

1 tsp paprika powder

2 tsp all-purpose seasoning

1 tsp apple cider vinegar

1 onion, chopped

4 garlic cloves, minced

3 tsp fish seasoning

3 sprigs spring onion

4 tomatoes, chopped

1 red pepper, sliced

540 g/ 1 can (19 oz) callaloo

salt and black pepper to taste

DIRECTIONS

To start drain banana blossom from can, pat dry with a paper towel and then mince into fine short strips. Transfer into a bowl and season with garlic powder, paprika, 2 tsp fish seasoning, apple cider vinegar and all 1 tsp purpose seasoning. Leave mixture to marinate for 30 minutes.

In a skillet over medium heat, add oil and seasoned banana blossom. Fry for 5 minutes and add a tsp salt whilst stirring.

Add chopped onions, spring onions, red pepper and tomatoes. Season with a tsp all-purpose seasoning and fish seasoning.

Drain callaloo and add to skillet, then combine together. Add black pepper and salt to taste.

Serve hot. Pair with fried dumplings, see recipe on page 77.

GOT A QUESTION ? ——————》

Plantain Pancakes

SERVES: 3   **COOK TIME:** 40 MINUTES   **DIFFICULTY:** ● ●

Rich in flavour with a delicious tender bite. Very similar to normal pancakes, with a sweet plantain undertone. Great for breakfast, but could easily double up for dessert. Don't hold back on toppings with this recipe. The sweet taste of plantain compliments so many different flavours from sweet syrups to fruit and nuts.

INGREDIENTS

3 over-ripe plantains

3 tbsp oil

187 g/ 1 ½ cups plain flour

244 g/ 1 cup plant based milk

113 g/ ½ cup vegan butter

1 tsp vanilla extract

1 tsp nutmeg

118 g/ ½ cup water

a pinch sea salt

Linseed egg:

1 tbsp ground flaxseed

3 tbsp hot water

Optional toppings:

nut butter

crushed hazelnuts

maple syrup

cinnamon

DIRECTIONS

Peel plantains and place into a large mixing bowl. Using a fork or a potato masher, mash until pureed and smooth.

Make linseed egg by combining flaxseed and hot water. Mix in a highspeed blender to form a gooey substance.

Add the rest of the ingredients to the blender and pulse until the ingredients have mixed thoroughly.

If you do not have a blender, mix ingredients together with a wooden spoon in a large mixing bowl until combined together well.

Leave the batter to set for approx. 30 minutes in a refrigerator.

Add oil to a non-stick frying pan and turn to medium heat. Slowly spoon mixture into pan and tilt to ensure it spreads over the entire pan. Cook pancakes thoroughly until golden brown.

Serve with nut butter, maple syrup and cinnamon. Feel free to add any of your favourite pancake toppings.

GOT A QUESTION ?
—————————»

Seasoned Beans

SERVES: 2   **COOK TIME:** 10 MINUTES   **DIFFICULTY:** ●

INGREDIENTS

1 tbsp plant-based butter

1 red pepper, chopped

400 g/ 1 can (15 oz) baked beans

1 tsp garlic powder

1 tsp onion powder

1 tsp paprika

½ tbsp oregano

black pepper and salt to taste

Optional toppings:

1 tbsp plain hummus

DIRECTIONS

Pre-heat skillet on a low heat and add butter. Once the butter has melted, add chopped red pepper and allow them to saute in the butter for 2 minutes with occasional stirring until soft.

Add the beans and simmer for 5 minutes with occasional stirring making sure the beans don't stick to the skillet.

Add onion powder, garlic powder, paprika, oregano and hummus. Mix together with beans.

Garnish with chopped coriander leaves and serve with other breakfast accompaniments.

GOT A QUESTION ?

Tofu Scramble

SERVES: 4   **COOK TIME:** 25 MINUTES   **DIFFICULTY:** ● ●

INGREDIENTS

225 g firm tofu

1 tbsp coconut oil

1 onion, chopped

1 tsp turmeric powder

1 tsp paprika

1 tbsp garlic powder

1 tsp kala namak/black salt

1 tsp cumin

Optional:

1 tsp cayenne or chilli powder

30 g/ 1 cup spinach, chopped

DIRECTIONS

Remove tofu from package and drain. Wrap the tofu in paper towel and apply pressure to press out remaining moisture. You can use a tofu press if you have one.

Using your hand, crumble your tofu into scrambled sized pieces and set aside.

In a large skillet, add oil and sauté onion for around 4 minutes on a medium to high heat.

Add tofu to sautéed onions.

Add turmeric, paprika, garlic powder, black salt, cumin and chilli powder.

Combine together and cook for 5 minutes. Add spinach and cook for a further 3 minutes. Serve with tomatoes, avocado and bread of choice.

 GOT A QUESTION ?

Vegan Tuna Melt

SERVES: 4   **COOK TIME:** 25 MINUTES   **DIFFICULTY:** ● ●

A healthy vegan seafood sandwich! Soft, delectable and satisfying. The chickpeas absorb the flavours immaculately and it's a great lunch idea. This definitely brings back some pleasurable childhood memories. We hope this recipe allows you to relive some old foodie moments from your past and make new moments right here and now.

INGREDIENTS

400 g/ 1 can (15 oz) chickpeas

2 shallots, minced

3 celery stalks, sliced

2 mini sweet peppers, roughly chopped

2 nori sheets, ground

2 tsp fish seasoning

1 tsp ground black pepper

2 tsp pimento powder

2 tbsp nutritional yeast

58 g/ ¼ cup vegan mayonnaise

2 tbsp relish

1 tsp sea salt

200 g vegan cheese

1 loaf bread

2 tbsp vegan butter

DIRECTIONS

Preheat oven to 200˚C/ 392˚F.

In a food processor, combine chickpeas, shallots, celery, sweet peppers and ground nori sheets. Pulse until smooth.

Spoon mixture into a bowl, add fish seasoning, black pepper, nutritional yeast, vegan mayo, relish and mix together. Set chickpea tuna aside.

Line a baking tray with foil. To make two sandwiches, butter the bread and turn upside down onto lined baking tray.

Spread chickpea tuna onto bread, add vegan cheese then a final layer of the chickpea mix. Cover sandwich butter side facing up and bake in oven for 10 minutes.

GOT A QUESTION ?

Being able to create and share special moments with good are the essentfeltsto a happy life

Dinner

The phrase **"Dinner is ready"** from a young age sparked a fierce competition between myself and my brother. In a game called "Who could get to the dinner table first!". There were no rules to this game, the main and only objective was to get to the dinner table first to ensure you get the biggest serving. Trick, trip and any form of martial arts we picked up from TV could be used in your arsenal to be the first to the table. Food definitely played a pivotal role in my childhood. All to say, I hope this section of **Eating good vegan** sparks the same interest I had when I was young and hope you can share this passion for food with your loved ones.

Ackee & Chickpea Curry

SERVES: 4   **COOK TIME:** 40 MINUTES   **DIFFICULTY:** ●●

This ackee and chickpea curry is the culmination of learning to cook at home, wanting to keep in shape and bringing our caribbean heritage together. It has formed this delicious protein packed, full of flavour recipe. The texture between the soft ackee and crunchy roasted chickpeas gives you a pleasurable mouthfeel experience. It's now your turn to get involved and try this new school recipe.

INGREDIENTS

400 g/ 1 can (15 oz) chickpeas soaked and cooked

1 tsp onion powder

1 tsp garlic powder

1 tsp paprika

1 tsp all-purpose seasoning

1 tsp oregano

1 tsp thyme

6 tbsp olive oil

1 large onion

5 garlic cloves, minced

2 large tomatoes, chopped

3 spring onions, diced

black pepper and salt to taste

1 tsp dried thyme

1 sweet red pepper, diced

½ leek, diced

400 g/ 1 can (15 oz) coconut milk

2 large tomatoes, chopped

400 g/ 1 can (15 oz) ackee

dill

DIRECTIONS

Pre-heat oven to 175°C/ 350°F.

Add chickpeas to a bowl with onion powder, garlic powder, paprika, allpurpose seasoning, oregano, thyme and olive oil. Combine together.

Spread chickpeas evenly on a lined baking tray and put to bake for 20 minutes until golden brown.

Add oil to a skillet over medium heat. Add onions, garlic, tomatoes and spring onions. Saute until tomatoes have lost most of their moisture. Add salt and black pepper and stir together.

Add sweet pepper, leeks and roasted chickpeas. Saute until leeks have softened. Add coconut milk, tomatoes and pimento powder. Stir and leave to simmer for 5 minutes. Add a splash of water to prevent the curry getting too thick.

Add ackee to pot and gently fold into the curry. Cover the pot and reduce to a low heat for 10 minutes before serving. Garnish with dill and toasted pine nuts.

GOT A QUESTION ? >>

Vegan BBQ Ribs

SERVES: 3   **COOK TIME:** 1 HOUR 40 MINUTES   **DIFFICULTY:** ● ● ●

The meatiest BBQ ribs! It has taste and texture like no other vegan ribs. From the stringy shredded oyster mushrooms combined with beyond meat juicy patties. This is a must-try recipe regardless of your dietary preferences. We can guarantee you will enjoy each and every bite that is filled with flavour and the texture is mind blowing. This recipe will certainly turn some heads with the sexy glazed coating and amazing aromas.

INGREDIENTS

2 mini peppers, chopped

1 celery stalk, chopped

1 medium onion, chopped

30 g jalapeno

2 garlic cloves, minced

200 g/ ½ can (15 oz) green young jackfruit, pulled roughly

1 king oyster mushrooms, pulled apart into strips

2 beyond meat patties, defrosted

1 tsp garlic powder

1 all-purpose seasoning

1 tsp smoked paprika

½ tsp liquid smoke

200ml BBQ sauce

DIRECTIONS

Preheat ovento 200˚C/ 392˚F.

Add all vegetables, except mushrooms and jackfruit to a food processor and mince together.

Spoon contents of food processor into a bowl and add jackfruit and mushrooms. Add thawed beyond meat burgers, garlic powder, allpurpose seasoning, smoked paprika and liquid smoke. Mix together well with your hands.

Line a baking tray and place contents of bowl onto the baking paper.

Press out into a rectangle and leave around 1 inch thick. Score rectangle into rib like strips about 2 inches wide.

Place in the oven for 45 minutes.

Remove from oven, slather barbecue on top and place back into the oven for a further 15 minutes.

GOT A QUESTION ? —————————»

Vegan Fried Calamari

SERVES: 4   **COOK TIME:** 1 HOUR 20 MINUTES   **DIFFICULTY:** ● ●

Before making the decision to go vegan, calamari was a real favourite and would be ordered at any restaurant that offered it. We've been experimenting with lots of different ingredients to make this dish as similar to the original as possible. Finally, we think we've cracked the code for the flavour and texture, it's simply amazing. This recipe will bring back memories of the good old days when calamari was on the menu.

INGREDIENTS

425 g/ 1 can (15 oz) hearts of palm

3 tbsp extra-virgin olive oil

1 nori sheet, ground

Wet batter:

125 g/ 1 cup flour

236 ml/ 1 cup water

1 tsp garlic powder

1 tsp onion powder

1 tsp all-purpose seasoning

1 tsp cajun seasoning

1 tsp salt

Dry batter:

138 g/ 1 cup cornmeal

31 g/ ¼ cup plain flour

1 tsp garlic powder

1 tsp onion powder

1 tsp all-purpose seasoning

1 tsp smoked paprika

1 tsp cajun seasoning

1 tsp dried parsley

DIRECTIONS

In a bowl, combine flour, water, garlic powder, onion powder, allpurpose seasoning, cajun seasoning, ground nori and salt. Mix together well.

Remove center of hearts of palm by pushing them out with your finger or a straw if you have one available. Slice hearts of palm into ringlets and add to the bowl.

In a separate bowl, make your dry batter by combining cornmeal, flour, cajun seasoning, garlic powder, onion powder, all-purpose seasoning, parsley and smoked paprika. Mix together well.

Gradually add marinated hearts of palm to dry mix and combine together.

Add oil to a skillet over medium heat and fry hearts of palm until golden brown. Serve with a dip of choice.

GOT A QUESTION ? ——≫

Cheeseburger Pasta

SERVES: 3   **COOK TIME:** 1 HOUR 20 MINUTES   **DIFFICULTY:** ● ●

INGREDIENTS

3 tbsp olive oil

1 large white onion

3 cloves of garlic, minced

2 beyond meat patties

1 tbsp garlic powder

1 tbsp all-purpose seasoning

1 tsp smoked paprika

1 tsp mix herbs

pinch of salt

500 g tomato sauce

236 ml/ 1 cup non-dairy milk

710 ml/ 3 cups vegetable broth

500 g pasta (we used conchigle)

4 tbsp nutritional yeast

83 g/ 1 cup applewood vegan cheese

Optional toppings:

handful grated cheese

DIRECTIONS

In a skillet over medium heat, add olive oil, onions and garlic. Saute until soft.

Add beyond meat patties to skillet and continue to fry. Add garlic powder, allpurpose seasoning, paprika, mixed herbs, salt and combine together.

Add tomato sauce, non-dairy milk, vegetable broth and pasta to pan and leave to cook for 10 minutes. Stir occasionally to prevent pasta from sticking.

Add nutritional yeast and vegan cheese mix together well and cook for a further 2 minutes.

Remove from heat and serve warm.

GOT A QUESTION ?
————————»

Vegan 'Salmon' Cakes

SERVES: 3   **COOK TIME:** 1 HOUR 20 MINUTES   **DIFFICULTY:** ● ●

Vegan salmon cakes. The search is over! This recipe caught your eye and here's why. It's suitable for lunch, brunch or dinner bringing you vibrant seafood flavours and joy. Make this recipe extra special with a coconut greek yogurt and top with a lemon wedge. It's easy to store, reheat or freeze but we doubt you'll have time to freeze these moreish vegan seafood delights.

INGREDIENTS

Salmon cakes

2 medium potatoes, sliced

2 tsp all purpose seasoning

473 ml/ 2 cups water

1 tsp butter

2 king oyster mushrooms stripped

400 g/ 1 can (14 oz) banana blossom

1 sheet nori, ground

½ lemon juice

1 tbsp garlic powder

2 tsp fish seasoning

salt and black pepper to taste

3 tbsp oil for frying

Garlic butter:

4 tbsp non-dairy butter

6 cloves garlic, minced

1 tsp lemon pepper seasoning

DIRECTIONS

Add potatoes and 1 tsp all purpose seasoning to water and leave to boil until softened, about 10 minutes.

Drain water from potatoes and add to a bowl. Add butter and mash until smooth. Add oyster mushrooms, banana blossom, nori, all purpose seasoning, lemon juice, garlic powder, fish seasoning, black pepper and salt to the bowl. Combine ingredients and shape into patties about 1 inch thick.

In a skillet add oil and shallow fry patties until crispy. Remove patties and place on kitchen towel to remove excess oil.

To make garlic butter, add vegan butter and garlic to skillet and saute for 8 minutes on a medium heat. Transfer to a container and brush or pour onto salmon cakes.

GOT A QUESTION ? ——»

Jerk Lentils

SERVES: 3   **COOK TIME:** 40 MINUTES   **DIFFICULTY:** ● ●

Jerk spices are certainly one of our favourite flavours and it's nostalgia is simply unmatched. We're all familiar with how jerk seasoning has been used on different meats but did you know that you can get super creative with it for plant-based dishes too. There's no better example than this jerk lentil recipe, where the lentils absorb the flavours really well which creates a seriously tasty dish.

INGREDIENTS

3 tbsp olive oil

1 onions

3 garlic cloves

1 scotch bonnet

2 thyme sprigs

½ tbsp cumin

½ tbsp all-spice

1 tbsp jerk seasoning

1 cinnamon stick

400 g/ 1 can (14 oz) chopped tomatoes

236 ml/ 1 cup vegetable broth

400 g lentils

1 tbsp maple syrup

DIRECTIONS

To a pre-heated skillet over a medium heat add oil to the pan with onions, garlic, scotch bonnet and thyme. Sauté until until the onions have softened.

Add cumin, all spice, jerk seasoning, cinnamon stick, chopped tomatoes, vegetable broth and lentils.

Cover and cook on a medium to high heat for 25 minutes.

Remove from the heat and set aside for 5 minutes before serving.

GOT A QUESTION ?
⟫

Lemon Pepper Cauliflower Wings

SERVES: 3   **COOK TIME:** 40 MINUTES   **DIFFICULTY:** ● ● ●

INGREDIENTS

lemon pepper seasoning:

¼ cup lemon zest, from 6 lemons

1 tbsp black pepper

1 tbsp sea salt

1 tsp garlic powder

1 tsp onion powder

1 tsp dried thyme

230 g/ 2 cups breadcrumbs

32 g/ ¼ cup lemon pepper, seasoning

236 ml/ 1 cup non-dairy milk

96 g/ ¾ cup all-purpose flour

1 head cauliflower

lemon pepper butter:

4 tbsp vegan butter

1 tbsp agave

4 tbsp lemon pepper seasoning

DIRECTIONS

Pre-heat oven to 230°C/ 450°F.

Combine lemon zest, black pepper, ground sea salt, onion powder, garlic powder and thyme to create lemon pepper seasoning.

In a bowl, combine bread crumbs, 3 tbsp of total amount of lemon pepper seasoning then mix together to make a dry mix.

In a separate container, combine almond milk, plain flour, 2 tbsp lemon pepper seasoning and mix together to make a wet mix.

Break cauliflower into florets and dip into wet mix, followed by dry mix and coat well.

On a lined baking tray, place cauliflower pieces and put to bake for 35 minutes.

To make lemon pepper butter, melt vegan butter, and combine with 1 tsp lemon pepper seasoning and agave.

Drizzle lemon pepper butter over baked cauliflower and serve hot.

GOT A QUESTION ? ——»

Pineapple Mac & Cheese

SERVES: 3   **COOK TIME:** 1 HOUR 20 MINUTES   **DIFFICULTY:** ● ● ●

Mac n cheese adorned with pineapple chunks, yes you are reading this correctly. If you like pineapples on pizza this Mac n cheese is going to blow your mind. This odd combination compliments each other to perfection. satisfying the bodily urges for sweet and salty food in one recipe.We definitely had our creative hats on for this recipe, join us in experiencing something we would like to call magical.

INGREDIENTS

1 tbsp onion powder

2 tbsp garlic powder

1 tbsp all purpose seasoning

3 tbsp extra-virgin olive oil

salt and black pepper to taste

550 g/ 6 cups conchiglie pasta

2 tbsp vegan butter

1 medium onion, chopped

4-6 garlic cloves, minced

125 g/ 1 cup all-purpose flour

400 ml/ 1 can (14 oz) vegan evaporated milk (or non-dairy milk)

30 g/ ½ cup nutritional yeast

1 tsp paprika powder

1 red pepper, chopped

200 g vegan red leicester cheese, shredded

200 g vegan mature cheddar cheese, shredded

400 g pineapples

200 g breadcrumbs

DIRECTIONS

Pre-heat oven to 200˚C/ 392˚F.

Bring a large pot ¾ full water to a boil. Add onion powder, garlic powder, all purpose seasoning, salt and black pepper. Add pasta to pot with olive oil and cook for approx. 7 minutes before straining and setting aside.

Add vegan butter to a skillet over a medium heat. Add onions, garlic and saute until translucent. Add 1 cup of flour and mix until lumpy for approx. 1 minute. Add vegan evaporated milk and combine.

Stir in nutritional yeast, 2 tsp garlic powder, 1 tsp paprika and a pinch of salt and black pepper.

Add sweet peppers to skillet followed by vegan cheese. Stir to combine.

Add pasta to a large baking tray. Pour contents in skillet over pasta and combine until evenly spread. Add pineapples to the baking tray and mix.

Add breadcrumbs as the top layer on the baking tray and put to bake for approx. 45-60 minutes. Serve hot.

GOT A QUESTION ? ——————»

Portobello Mushroom Steak

SERVES: 1   **COOK TIME:** 30 MINUTES   **DIFFICULTY:** ●

Steak lovers, you have just found the holy grail for a mouthwateringly meaty vegan steak. Tender and juicy, these pan seared portobello mushrooms are hearty and more than enough for meat lovers, perfect for a fantastic vegan option for your chosen meatless day of the week.

INGREDIENTS

2 tbsp melted butter

1 tsp all purpose seasoning

1 tsp garlic powder

1 tsp liquid smoke

2 tsp soy sauce

2 tbsp maple syrup

6 garlic cloves

3 sprigs rosemary leaves

1 large portobello mushroom

black pepper and salt

DIRECTIONS

In a bowl combine melted butter with all purpose seasoning, garlic powder, liquid smoke, soy sauce and maple syrup. Add mushroom to bowl and coat well with marinade. Set aside for 10 minutes.

In a skillet over medium heat, melt 1 tbsp butter. Add whole garlic cloves to pan alongside rosemary. Add mushroom to pan to sear. Add pressure to mushroom when searing both sides.

Add a pinch of black pepper and salt and serve mushrooms with accompaniment of choice. This pairs well with creamy mash potatoes and green peas.

 GOT A QUESTION ?

Vegan Philly Cheese Steak

SERVES: 4 **COOK TIME:** 1 HOUR 20 MINUTES **DIFFICULTY:** ● ● ●

INGREDIENTS

400 g/ 1 can (14 oz) black beans

180 g/ 1 ½ cups vital wheat gluten flour

1 tsp all purpose seasoning

4 tbsp nutritional yeast

1 tsp garlic powder

1 tsp paprika

1 tsp dried oregano

1 tsp sea salt

1 tsp black pepper

118 ml/ ½ cup water

1 tbsp extra-virgin olive oil

1 onion

2 bell peppers

2 chilli peppers

50 g vegan cheese

2 baguettes

Optional toppings:

vegan mayo

BBQ sauce

DIRECTIONS

Drain and mash black beans in a bowl until they have turned into a paste.

Add vital wheat gluten flour, all purpose seasoning, nutritional yeast, garlic powder, paprika, oregano, salt, black pepper. Combine together and then add water gradually whilst kneading mixture together to make your vegan meat.

Once your vegan meat dough has come together, slice into 1 inch thick strips and set aside.

Add oil to a skillet on medium heat and saute onions, bell peppers, chilli peppers for 5 minutes, then set aside.

To a separate pan, add more olive oil and fry vegan meat pieces for 10 minutes, then set aside.

Toast your bread for a couple minutes in the oven. Assemble cheese steak by adding sauce of choice to base of bread, then layering vegan meat pieces and sauteed vegetables on top.

In a skillet, add a dash of oil on a medium heat and melt vegan cheese before adding to assembled cheese steak.

GOT A QUESTION ?
———»

BBQ Vegan Pulled Pork Burger

SERVES: 4   **COOK TIME:** 55 MINUTES   **DIFFICULTY:** ● ● ●

INGREDIENTS

4 king oyster mushrooms, sliced

1 tsp all purpose seasoning

1 tsp smoked paprika

3 tbsp jerk paste

3 tbsp olive oil

2 medium onions

5 garlic cloves, diced

400 g/ 1 can (15 oz) young green jackfruit

200 ml hot water

1 vegetable stock

300 ml BBQ sauce

DIRECTIONS

Pre-heat oven TO 200°C/ 392°F.

In a bowl combine sliced king oyster mushrooms, all purpose seasoning and smoked paprika. Mix together well. Transfer mushrooms to a lined baking tray and cook for 20 minutes.

Remove baked oyster mushrooms from oven and using two forks, pull them apart into strips. Set aside.

Drain jack fruit from can. Place pieces onto a chopping boards and remove hard ends. Roughly pull jackfruit apart and set aside with mushrooms.

In a skillet on medium heat, add oil, onions and garlic and saute for 3 minutes. add jackfruit vegetable stock, mushrooms, and BBQ sauce. Cook on a medium heat for a couple of minutes to reduce liquid. Transfer mix to a lined baking tray and bake for 10 minutes.

Remove mix from oven. Serve with burger buns, vegan coleslaw and any other toppings of your choice.

GOT A QUESTION ? ——≫

Rasta Pasta

SERVES: 3   **COOK TIME:** 45 MINUTES   **DIFFICULTY:** ● ●

This is hands down one of our favourite dishes. It's an easy recipe inspired by the traditional Rasta Pasta made with chicken. We made jerk flavoured King Oyster Mushrooms to replace the chicken which brings incredible flavour and texture to the dish. It's also super creamy, 'cheesy' and vibrant, made with coconut milk, nutritional yeast and different coloured sweet peppers.

INGREDIENTS

450g king oyster mushrooms

2 tsp olive oil

1 tsp chicken seasoning

1 tsp onion powder

1 tsp garlic powder

1 tsp paprika

1 tsp all-purpose seasoning

1 tsp black pepper

1 tbsp jerk paste

1 sprig spring onion, sliced

5 garlic cloves, minced

3 whole sweet peppers (red, green & orange)

1 tsp thyme

1 tsp apple cider vinegar

2 cups coconut milk

1 ½ cups non-dairy cheese

½ cup nutritional yeast

1 tsp dry jerk seasoning

2 tbsp non-dairy butter

500g cooked penne pasta

DIRECTIONS

Pre-heat oven to 200˚C/ 392˚F.

On a chopping board, slice the oyster mushrooms and pull using end of a fork. Add the strips to a bowl. Add olive oil, chicken seasoning, onion powder, garlic powder, paprika, all-purpose seasoning, black pepper and jerk paste. Mix together till strips are coated well.

Spread the marinated oyster mushrooms onto a lined baking tray and put to bake for 15 minutes.

In a skillet over medium heat, add oil, spring onions, garlic, sweet peppers and saute for 5 minutes. Add baked mushroom pieces, followed by coconut milk and stir together. Leave to cook for 10 minutes.

Cook pasta according to instructions on the packet. Drain water and add to skillet.

Add non-dairy cheese, nutritional yeast, jerk seasoning and butter. Mix together well and cook for a further 5 minutes.

Serve hot.

GOT A QUESTION ?

Vegan Fried Chicken

SERVES: 4   **COOK TIME:** 1 HOUR 20 MINUTES   **DIFFICULTY:** ● ● ●

INGREDIENTS

236 ml/ 1 cup almond milk

1 tsp lemon juice

1 tbsp aquafaba

1 tbsp hot sauce (optional)

500 g cluster oyster mushrooms

240 g/ 2 cup plain white flour

2 tsp sea salt

1 tbsp garlic powder

1 tbsp onion powder

2 tsp black pepper

2 tsp smoked paprika

2 tsp cajun seasoning

250 ml/ 2 cup oil for frying

DIRECTIONS

To a bowl add almond milk, lemon juice and aquafaba. Whisk ingredients together to create a buttermilk. Add hot sauce and combine.

In a separate bowl, add oyster mushrooms and break roughly apart, leaving large clumps together. Pour buttermilk mixture over oyster mushrooms. Coat roughly and cover bowl with cling film. Set aside for at least 20 minutes.

In another bowl, mix flour, sea salt, garlic powder, onion powder, black pepper, paprika and cajun seasoning.

Add the marinated oyster mushroom pieces individually to the flour, then back into the marinade and once again coat in the flour mix.

Place the coated oyster mushroom pieces on a wire rack and allow them to dry for 10 to 15 minutes.

In a pan or deep fryer, fry oyster mushroom pieces on a medium to high heat until golden and crispy. Allow each fried oyster mushroom piece to drain any excess oil on a paper towel beneath a wire wrack. Serve whilst still hot.

GOT A QUESTION ? ————————»

Jamaican Style Stew Peas

SERVES: 4   **COOK TIME:** 1 HOUR 20 MINUTES   **DIFFICULTY:** ● ● ●

INGREDIENTS

200g soy chunks, hydrated

4 tbsp extra-virgin olive oil

1 red onion, chopped

4 cloves garlic, minced

1 carrot, sliced

3 tsp salt

800 g/ 2 cans (15 oz) cooked kidney beans

400 ml/ 1 can (15 oz) coconut milk

1 tbsp garlic powder

½ tbsp onion powder

½ tbsp pimento powder

1 tsp paprika

½ tbsp all purpose seasoning

236 ml/ 1 cup hot water

1 vegetable stock cube

1 spring onion

3 sprigs thyme

1 scotch bonnet

Spinners

1 cup all purpose flour

118 ml/ ½ cup water

DIRECTIONS

Hydrate soy chunks by adding them to a bowl and filling with cold water. Set aside and leave for 25 minutes.

In a saucepan over medium heat, add oil, onions, garlic and carrots. Saute for 5 minutes until onions are translucent.

Drain soy chunks and press to remove as much water as possible. Add soy chunks to the skillet. Add tsp salt and a little more oil to pan if required, leave to cook for 15 minutes whilst stirring occasionally.

Add canned kidney beans to pan followed by coconut milk.

Add garlic powder, onion powder, pimento powder, paprika and all purpose seasoning to saucepan then mix together.

Combine hot water with vegetable stock cube then add to saucepan.

Add spring onion, thyme and scotch bonnet and turn to a low to medium heat.

Make spinners by adding flour to bowl, 1 tsp salt and water. Mix together to form a dough. Pinch a small piece of dough into hands and roll together to make spinners. Add to saucepan and turn to a medium to high heat. Cook for 25 minutes.

Serve with rice.

GOT A QUESTION ? ——»

Red Beans & Rice

SERVES: 2   **COOK TIME:** 45 MINUTES   **DIFFICULTY:** ● ●

INGREDIENTS

1 tbsp extra-virgin olive oil

4 vegan sausages, sliced

1 onion, chopped

4 garlic cloves, minced

1 green bell pepper, sliced

2 celery stalks, sliced

salt and black pepper to taste

800 ml/ 3 ½ cup hot water

1 vegetable stock cube

1 can (15 oz) kidney beans

1 tbsp cajun seasoning

1 tbsp garlic powder

1 tsp paprika

1 tsp mixed herbs

1 tsp apple cider vinegar

2 bay leaves

2 sprigs fresh thyme

DIRECTIONS

Add oil to a skillet and fry sausages until browned. Add onions, garlic, bell pepper, celery, and salt. Saute until sweet pepper have started to brown.

Combine hot water with the vegetable stock cube. Add to pan, followed by kidney beans, cajun seasoning, garlic powder, paprika, mixed herbs, apple cider vinegar, bay leaves, and thyme. Cover and leave to cook for 35 minutes.

Serve hot with rice.

GOT A QUESTION ? ——»

Vegan Salisbury Steak

SERVES: 2   **COOK TIME:** 45 MINUTES   **DIFFICULTY:** ● ●

This is a go-to meal for us and it's always a hit with family and friends. It's incredibly flavoursome and the texture of the steak is ideal. This recipe is the perfect meal for any day of the week, it's quick and easy to put together cooked down in simple and delicious gravy.

INGREDIENTS

2 onions, sliced

1 shallot, sliced

50 g/ ½ cup walnuts, roughly, chopped

4 cloves garlic, minced

3 mini sweet peppers, sliced and seeded

4 beyond meat patties, defrosted

2 tbsp all-purpose seasoning

1 tbsp garlic powder

1 tsp paprika

½ tsp chilli flakes

60 g/ ½ cup breadcrumbs

1 tsp salt

1 tsp black pepper

4 tbsp extra-virgin olive oil

4 tbsp plain flour

450 ml/ 2 cups water

1 tsp browning

1 tbsp tomato sauce

DIRECTIONS

In a food processor, add 1 onion, shallot, garlic, sweet peppers and pulse until well combined.

Spoon mixture from food processor into a bowl and add thawed beyond meat patties, all-purpose seasoning, garlic powder, paprika, chilli flakes, breadcrumbs, salt and black pepper. Mix together and assemble into round 1 inch thick patties.

Add oil to a skillet on medium heat and fry patties until browned on each side. Remove patties from the skillet and set aside.

In the same skillet, add some more oil, followed by 1 onion and leave to saute for 3 minutes. Add flour and water and stir together to prevent lumps being formed. Stir in all-purpose seasoning, browning and tomato sauce.

Return patties to skillet and cover with a lid. Cook for a further 15 minutes on a low to medium heat.

GOT A QUESTION ?

Tofu & Plantain Curry

SERVES: 4   **COOK TIME:** 35 MINUTES   **DIFFICULTY:** ● ●

INGREDIENTS

2 tbsp extra-virgin olive oil

5 shallots, diced

5 garlic gloves, minced

300 g red thai curry paste

400 g extra-firm tofu, drained and chopped into blocks

2 tbsp soy sauce

400 ml/ 1 can (14 oz) coconut milk

1 tsp all purpose seasoning

2 tbsp sugar

1 tsp smoked paprika

2 bay leaves

1 head broccoli, chopped into florets

1 red pepper, chopped

1 tsp salt

2 tbsp chopped parsley

1 ripe plantain, sliced

½ lime, squeezed

DIRECTIONS

In a skillet on medium heat, add oil, chopped shallots, garlic and saute for 3 minutes. Add red Thai curry paste to pan followed by sliced and drained tofu.

Add soy sauce, coconut milk, all purpose seasoning, sugar, smoked paprika, bay leaves, broccoli, red pepper, salt, parsley and leave to cook for 10 minutes on a medium heat. Add sliced plantain pan followed by lime juice and leave to cook for a further 10 minutes.

Serve hot with rice.

GOT A QUESTION ? ——————»

Curried Tofu

SERVES: 4   **COOK TIME:** 45 MINUTES   **DIFFICULTY:** ● ●

INGREDIENTS

400 g extra-firm tofu, drained and sliced

4 tbsp extra-virgin olive oil

2 tbsp chicken seasoning

1 tsp black pepper

1 tsp salt

1 tbsp butter

1 tbsp minced garlic

1 tbsp turmeric

1 large onion

2 medium tomatoes

1 bell pepper

2 stalks spring onions, chopped

2 potatoes, peeled and sliced

5 springs thyme

1 scotch bonnet

400 ml/ 1 can (14 oz) coconut milk

3 tbsp apple cider vinegar

1 tbsp garlic powder

1 tsp onion powder

1 tbsp all purpose seasoning

1 tsp pimento

DIRECTIONS

Slice tofu into cubes and put in a large mixing bowl. Add olive oil, chicken seasoning, black pepper and salt. Gently combine to coat the tofu pieces.

To a skillet over a medium heat, add oil, butter, garlic, turmeric and combine.

Next add onions, tomatoes, bell pepper, spring onions, potatoes, scotch bonnet, thyme, coconut milk and apple cider vinegar. Season by adding garlic powder, onion powder, chicken seasoning, all purpose seasoning, pimento, black pepper and mix together.

Cover pan with lid and cook on medium heat for 25 minutes.

Add the marinated tofu pieces and stir. Cover again and cook for a further 5 minutes before serving.

Serve hot with rice.

GOT A QUESTION ? ———》

Vegan Curry Goat

SERVES: 5   **COOK TIME:** 1 HOUR 30 MINUTES   **DIFFICULTY:** ● ● ● ●

Curry Goat is a Caribbean staple. For the first time, with this recipe we have put together for you, you can enjoy this intensely delicious and tasty meal, only vegan! What a time to be alive. We made the "goat" pieces with homemade seitan complimented with a range of spices that unlocks a world of flavour. It can take some elbow grease to put your meat pieces together, but it's worth it, trust me! This dish has an authentic Caribbean flavour and texture profile, it will leave you speechless.

INGREDIENTS

Vegan Goat Meat:

250 g/ 1 ¼ cup cooked
brown lentils

180 g/ 1 ½ cup vital wheat gluten

2 tbsp nutritional yeast

1 tbsp garlic powder

1 tbsp onion powder

2 tsp coriander powder

1 tbsp allpurpose seasoning

1 tsp chilli powder

1 tsp nutmeg

1 tsp salt and black pepper

118 ml/ ½ cup water

Curry:

2 tbsp coconut oil

2 onion, diced

4 garlic cloves, minced

2 tbsp curry powder

1 tsp pimento powder

2 bell peppers, red and green, chopped

1 sweet potato, peeled and sliced

3 sprigs thyme

1 bay leaf

½ spring onion

1 scotch bonnet

470 ml/ 2 cups vegetable broth

Vegan
Curry Goat

DIRECTIONS

In a bowl, add cooked brown lentils and roughly mash. Add remaining vegan goat meat ingredients and combine together. Add water gradually and make it into a dough. Knead together well for approx. 5 minutes. When your meat dough is firmly together, cut it into 1 inch x 1 inch meaty pieces and set aside.

In a skillet over medium-high heat, fry onions and garlic until they become soft. Add curry powder, pimento powder, and seitan pieces to skillet and fry and stir to combine.

Add sweet peppers, sweet potatoes and continue to fry, add more oil if required.

Add thyme, bay leaf, spring onion, scotch bonnet and vegetable broth.

Cook for 35 minutes on low to medium heat whilst mix thickens. Add a little more water if necessary. Don't let mixture dry out. Add black pepper and salt to taste.

Serve hot.

When the food hits, the moments never miss

Vegan Jambalaya

SERVES: 4   **COOK TIME:** 1 HOUR 10 MINUTES   **DIFFICULTY:** ● ● ● ○

INGREDIENTS

100 g soy chunks, hydrated

2 tbsp extra-virgin olive oil

4 vegan sausages, sliced

1 onion, chopped

5 garlic cloves, minced

2 celery sticks, chopped

2 spring onions, sliced

2 green bell peppers, chopped

1 red chilli sliced

1 tbsp garlic powder

2 tbsp cajun seasoning

1 bay leaf

2 tsp dried thyme

400 g/2 cups long-grain rice, washed and drained

400 g/1 can (14 oz) chopped tomatoes

700 ml/3 cups vegetable broth

1 tsp paprika

1 tsp all purpose seasoning

1 tsp cayenne pepper

black pepper and salt to taste

1 ripe fried plantain

DIRECTIONS

Submerge soy chunks in water and set aside for 30 minutes until they hydrate before draining.

In a skillet, add oil and fry vegan sausages with soy chunks until browned to make a vegan meat mix. Place vegan meat mix aside.

Add more oil to the skillet and saute onions, garlic, celery, spring onions bell peppers and chilli. Add garlic powder, cajun seasoning, bay leaves and thyme. Add vegan meat mix back to the pan. Add rice, chopped tomatoes and vegetable broth.

Add paprika, all purpose seasoning, cayenne pepper, salt and black pepper. Leave to cook until rice becomes fluffy and liquid has reduced.

In a separate skillet, slice and fry one plantain before adding to jambalaya and mix together. Serve hot.

GOT A QUESTION ? ——»

Carribean Jackfruit Curry

SERVES: 4   **COOK TIME:** 45 MINUTES   **DIFFICULTY:** ● ●

Jackfruit is fantastically stringy, so it is an ideal swap for meat like pulled pork or shredded chicken. This curry is full of flavour, warmth and hearty goodness. This is definitely a staple recipe we come back to time and time again. Jackfruit, with its meaty texture, easy absorption and subtle sweetness, makes for an excellent curry.

INGREDIENTS

Curry paste:

1 onion, chopped

thumb-sized piece fresh ginger

4 garlic cloves

2 spring onions

2 tbsp vegetable oil

1 tsp ground turmeric

2 tbsp madras curry powder

1 tbsp tomato purée

2 large tomatoes, chopped

5 small potatoes, chopped

2 carrots, chopped

2 tbsp garlic powder

1 tsp allspice

1 tsp all purpose seasoning

1 tbsp soy sauce

500ml vegetable stock

400 g/ 1 can (14oz) can black eyed beans, drained and rinsed

800 g/ 2 cans (14 oz) young jackfruit in water, drained and rinsed

pinch freshly ground black pepper

4 fresh thyme sprigs

1 scotch bonnet chilli, seeded

DIRECTIONS

Add curry paste ingredients to a food processor and blend together.

In a large non-stick skillet, heat oil over a medium heat. Add curry paste, turmeric, curry powder and tomato puree. Combine together on a low to medium heat for 3 minutes.

Add tomatoes, potatoes and carrots to pan and combine together. Add garlic powder, allspice, all purpose seasoning and soy sauce and mix together well.

Combine hot water and vegetable stock and add to pan. Add blackeyed beans, jackfruit and mix together well. Add black pepper, thyme and scotch bonnet then bring to a boil for 20 minutes over a high heat.

Use a wooden spoon to squash and separate pieces of jackfruit into strips.

Serve hot. Goes well with coconut rice, find coconut rice recipe on page 75.

GOT A QUESTION ?

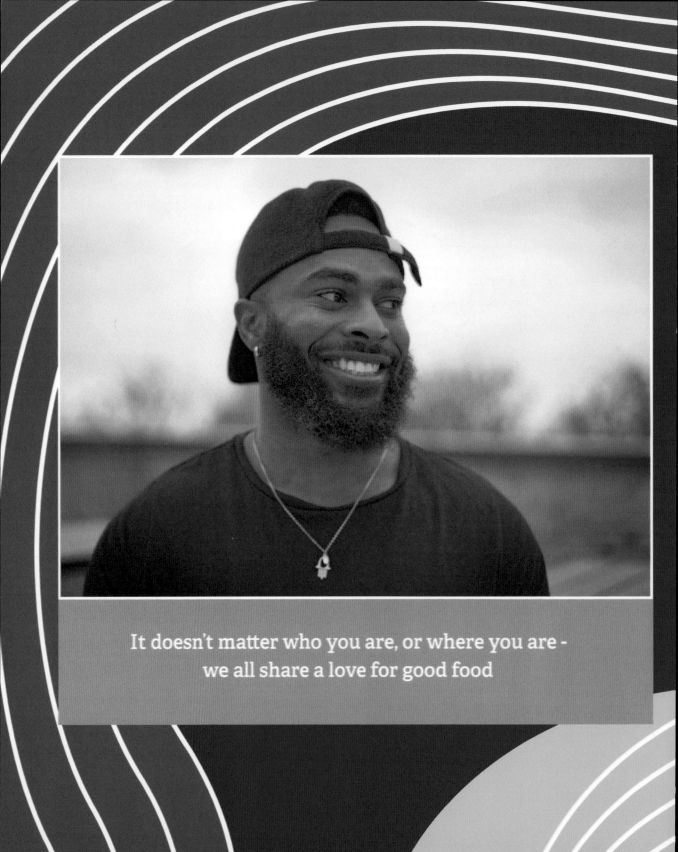

It doesn't matter who you are, or where you are -
we all share a love for good food

Side

Is it just us? But we believe sides can steal the show and transform your whole meal altogether. This selection of sides will do exactly that. If anything doesn't turn out how it was supposed to, don't worry, it's prone to happen sooner or later. Just remember, that's all part of the fun when **getting creative in the kitchen.** Rest easy though, because we've tried and tested each recipe with friends and family and they all passed the taste test. Yes! Once we had the sign of approval we knew they were ready for **Eating Good Vegan.**

Garlic & Broccoli

SERVES: 2   **COOK TIME:** 20 MINUTES   **DIFFICULTY:** ●

INGREDIENTS

1 head broccoli

4 tbsp extra-virgin olive oil

1 tsp maple syrup

1 tsp tamari

10 garlic cloves, diced

1 tsp all-purpose seasoning

½ tsp black pepper

a pinch salt

DIRECTIONS

Wash and chop broccoli into florets.

Over a medium to high heat, boil water and place broccoli above pan in a heat resistant colander for 4 minutes to steam. Remove broccoli from heat and use cold water to rinse.

In a separate skillet over a medium heat, add oil, tamari and maple syrup, then mix together. Add chopped garlic and saute for a couple minutes.

Add broccoli to skillet, with all-purpose seasoning, black pepper, salt and mix together.

Serve hot.

GOT A QUESTION ? ——————》

Coconut Rice

SERVES: 4   **COOK TIME:** 25 MINUTES   **DIFFICULTY:** ●●

INGREDIENTS

585 g/ 3 cups basmati rice, washed

400 ml/ 1 can (14 oz) coconut milk

2 garlic cloves, minced

1 tsp dried thyme

1 tbsp maple syrup

½ tsp salt

DIRECTIONS

Add rice to a saucepan and add water till it is around 1 cm above rice.

Turn to a high heat. Add coconut milk, garlic, thyme, maple syrup, salt and mix together.

Once pot is boiling, fluff rice and reduce heat to low before placing lid on top to allow to steam and cook through for a further 15 minutes.

Remove rice from heat, fluff again before serving hot.

GOT A QUESTION ? ——»

Fried Dumplings

SERVES: 4   **COOK TIME:** 25 MINUTES   **DIFFICULTY:** ● ●

Crispy on the outside and perfectly soft in the middle. Fried dumplings are a popular Jamaican dish that can be eaten for breakfast, lunch or dinner. It is a Caribbean favourite that can truly be eaten with just about anything. Made with a couple ingredients and easy and simple to put together.

INGREDIENTS

250 g/ 2 cups flour

1 tsp baking powder

2 tsp salt

2 tbsp butter

118 ml/ ½ cup non-dairy milk

78 ml/ ⅓ cup olive oil

DIRECTIONS

In a mixing bowl, add flour, baking powder, salt and butter. Combine together roughly with hands.

Gradually add non-dairy milk to bowl and make the mixture into a dough. Add more flour if your dough is too sticky.

Remove dough ball from the bowl and continue to knead on a flat floured surface.

Cover dough ball with cling film and leave to rest in the fridge for 30 minutes.

Remove dough from the fridge and make into round dumplings.

Add oil to non-stick skillet over medium heat. When oil is hot, add dumplings and fry until golden brown on both sides.

Remove dumplings from oil and place on kitchen towels to drain excess oil before serving.

GOT A QUESTION ?
——————»

Rice & Peas

SERVES: 4   **COOK TIME:** 40 MINUTES   **DIFFICULTY:** ●●

Growing up, it was tradition to make Rice and Peas every Sunday, for events and special occasions. It's a staple and an essential recipe which is the perfect compliment to a range of meals whether you're cooking a traditional Caribbean feast or otherwise. Made with kidney beans, basmati rice, coconut cream, fragrant spices and scotch bonnet.

INGREDIENTS

800 g/ 2 can (14 oz) cooked kidney beans

100 ml water

200 g creamed coconut

1 onion, chopped

6 garlic cloves, minced

3 sprigs fresh thyme

1 spring onion

1 scotch bonnet

1 tsp salt

1 tsp black pepper

500 g long grain rice, washed and drained

DIRECTIONS

Over a medium heat, add kidney beans to a saucepan, with water and creamed coconut and bring to a boil, mix together until creamed coconut has reduced.

Add onions, garlic, thyme, spring onion, scotch bonnet, salt and black pepper to saucepan. Add rice to saucepan and mix well together.

Cover mixture and boil on a high heat for 7 minutes until liquid starts reducing.

When liquid has reduced, turn to lowest heat and leave to steam with lid on pan for 20 - 25 minutes.

Fluff rice with a fork and leave to sit for a couple minutes before serving hot.

GOT A QUESTION ? ──────≫

Quick Jerk Hummus

SERVES: 4   **COOK TIME:** 15 MINUTES   **DIFFICULTY:** ●

INGREDIENTS

120 g/ ½ cup tahini

53 g/ ¼ cup olive oil

400 g/ 1 can (14 oz) cooked chickpeas

4 tbsp ice cold water

57 g/ ¼ cup lime juice

1 tbsp ground cumin powder

1 tsp brown sugar

1 tsp jerk paste

1 tsp soya milk (optional)

DIRECTIONS

Add, tahini, olive oil to a food processor and blend together.

Add remaining ingredients and blend until smooth.

For a creamier consistency, add soya milk and pulse until well combined.

GOT A QUESTION ? ——»

Sharing the pleasures of life, strengthens bonds
We can't think of anything more pleasureable than good food

Drinks

From dinners to drink recipes, in this section we've included some of our favourites. These are recipes that are always present in times of celebration, whether it is at a family gathering at Christmas, at a party or carnival. These drinks will **add more flavour and enjoyment to your occasions**, whether you make them virgin or not. Give them a try and see for yourself.

Please take the time to read through the recipes and follow each recipe step by step, this would mean alot to us. We've poured a lot of time and effort to ensure the flavours are perfect.

Rum Punch

SERVES: 4   **COOK TIME:** 15 MINUTES   **DIFFICULTY:** ●

INGREDIENTS

236 ml/ 1 cup white rum

236 ml/ 1 cup coconut rum

118 ml/ ½ cup lemon juice

handful pimento seeds

118 ml/ ½ cup strawberry or
raspberry syrup

470 ml/ 2 cups orange juice

470 ml/ 2 cup tropical juice

470 ml/ 2 cups pineapple juice

1 orange, thinly sliced

192 g/ 2 cups ginger, chopped

118 ml/ ½ cup wine (optional)

DIRECTIONS

In a jug, add white rum, coconut rum, lemon juice, pimento seeds, syrup, orange juice, tropical juice, pineapple juice, and mix together.

Add sliced oranges and ginger to jug and stir together.

Pour mixture through a sieve to remove pimento seeds and fruits. Serve with ice.

Refrigerate remaining amount for up to a week.

GOT A QUESTION ? ——»

Sorrel Wine

SERVES: 4   **COOK TIME:** 50 MINUTES   **DIFFICULTY:** ●●

This popular Jamaican Sorrel wine is an incredible compliment to the festive season. A tart, sweet, tangy magenta coloured, glass of refreshment. Made fresh with dried sorrel, spices, rum and ginger wine. This is the perfect addition to your Christmas table.

INGREDIENTS

130 g/ 2 cups dried sorrel/hibiscus

1.4 l/ 6 cups water

236 ml/ 1 cup ginger wine

118 ml/ ½ cup white rum

200 g/ 1 cup brown sugar

2 tbsp lemon juice

150 g/ 1 ½ cups ginger, crushed or chopped into cubes

2 sticks cinnamon

3 bay leaves

handful pimento seeds

1 orange, peeled and sliced

1 lime, sliced

DIRECTIONS

Add sorrel/hibiscus to a saucepan with bay leaves, peel of orange, pimento seeds, 1 cup of half crushed ginger and hot water. Leave to simmer for 30 minutes. Remove from heat and leave to cool.

Blend rest of ginger with 1 cup water and strain into a jug. Discard remains from ginger.

Strain cooled sorrel mix into the same jug and discard used spices.

Add sugar, lemon juice, ginger wine, rum and mix together.

GOT A QUESTION ?
———————»

Join Us Here

We hope you're enjoying the recipes. We want this book to be as user-friendly as possible, so we want to invite you to join our community. Scan the QR code below and be sure to share your recreations. Also if you have any questions, we will be on hand to answer.

Printed in Great Britain
by Amazon

14688974R00051